FOOTSTEPS IN TIME

THE Plains People

Sally Hewitt

Contents

Children's Press
A Division of Grolier Publishing
New York • London • Hong Kong • Sydney
Danbury, Connecticut

The Plains Peoples

The vast Plains of North America - once called prairies - used to be completely covered with grass. Enormous herds of buffalo grazed there. Now wheat and corn grow there instead.

Many of the Plains people were hunters and nomads. They followed the buffalo herds, taking everything they owned with them. Others lived in villages, grew corn, beans, and squash, and only hunted buffalo in the summer.

The people belonged to tribes such as the Sioux, Blackfoot, Mandan, Pawnee, Cheyenne, and Comanche. They were led by a chief chosen for his wisdom and bravery.

The men were hunters and warriors while the women did most of the camp or village work. Parents taught their children the skills they would need when they grew up.

3

Picture stories

To record important tribal events, Plains Indians painted picture symbols on buffalo hides or deerskins.

Some symbols:

| Warrior | Buffalo | Deer | Rain clouds | Mountains |

You will need:

Felt-tip pens   Scissors   Paints
Cardboard   Pencil

Follow the steps . . .

1. Draw a deerskin shape on the cardboard. Paint it light brown. Let it dry, then cut it out.

2. Paint or draw Indian picture symbols on the deerskin to tell a story.

3. Now make up your own picture symbols to tell a story about yourself.

Porcupine quills

Flattened and dyed, porcupine quills were woven or braided into beautiful decorations for clothes.

You will need:

Straws   Paints   Ruler
Adhesive tape

Follow the steps . . .

1. Flatten the straws with the ruler. Paint some of the straws bright colors. Tape a row of white straws onto another white straw. Then weave the colored straws in and out.

2. Tape three different-colored straws at one end and braid them.

3. Wrap a colored straw around one of a different color.

Living with the buffalo

Buffalo provided the people of the Plains with nearly everything they needed. When a buffalo was killed, some of the meat was cooked and eaten. The rest was cut into strips, dried on racks and stored for the winter. The hide was pegged out on the ground, scraped clean, softened and then stretched on a frame to dry.

The women made clothes and moccasins (their shoes) from the hide. Whole skins were sewn together to make tents called tipis which were easy to take down when the tribe moved on. Buffalo horns were made into cups, bowls, and tools.

9

Tipi

It took more than 12 buffalo skins to make a tipi.
A family symbol was often painted on the door flap.

You will need:

Brown paper   Felt-tip pens   Adhesive tape
Four straws   Scissors   String

Follow the steps . . .

1. Draw a semi-circle like this
   on the brown paper and cut it out.

2. Crumple the paper and decorate
   it with patterns and pictures.

3. Bend the semi-circle into a cone
   and tape the edges together.

4. Tie the straws together,
   push them through the hole
   in the tipi, and tape them to the sides.
   Add a decorated flap.

Courage and warfare

Warfare was part of life on the Plains. Tribes fought over buffalo hunting grounds and raided each other's camps for horses.

Young men were trained to be strong and brave. Races and wrestling kept them fit, and they practiced riding and using bows and arrows.

Before going to war, warriors gained courage and strength by dancing to songs and drumbeats. They painted their bodies and their horses with colors and symbols representing spirits that would protect them.

Feather headdress

The feathers in a warrior's headdress represented his brave deeds in battle.

You will need:

White construction paper	Adhesive tape	Scissors
Red construction paper	Pencil	Paints
Strip of cardboard	Paints	

Follow the steps . . .

1. Fold strips of white paper in half. Draw half a feather shape on each strip. Cut them out.

2. Snip the edges of the feather shapes. Paint the tips brown. Wrap and tape red paper around the stem.

3. Cut the cardboard strip to fit around your head. Paint bright shapes on it. Tape the ends to make a headband. Tape three feathers to the back.

A shield

Warriors carried shields made of hardened buffalo hide. They had to earn the right to decorate them.

You will need:

A cardboard box   Adhesive tape   Paints

Scissors   Feathers (see page 16)

Follow the steps . . .

1. Cut a circle for your shield from the base of the cardboard box.

2. Paint your shield with symbols to give you strength and protect you in battle.

3. Make feathers as you did for for your headdress (page 16).

4. Cut a handle from the sides of the box and tape it to the back of your shield.

Changing way of life

The Plains people believed that the land belonged to everyone. They did not understand why settlers came from Europe and fought them for the land. The settlers plowed the land, grazed cattle on it, dug mines, built towns, and slaughtered the buffalo. The Plains people were forced to give up their way of life and live on small plots of land called reservations.

In modern America, many Plains people live on reservations. Others live and work in the cities, but they have not forgotten their religion, ceremonies, crafts, and skills.

Today, many tribes get together at powwows. They dress in their traditional clothes and sing, dance, and feast. The tribes are working together for a better future for their people.

Drum and drummer

An Indian drum is a sacred object. It is the heartbeat of the people.

You will need:

A cardboard box   Felt-tip pens   Scissors

A stick   Brown paper   Newspaper

String   Glue

Follow the steps . . .

1. Cut a circle from the base of the box. Snip and bend the edges.

2. Glue a strip of cardboard to the bent flaps around the circle.

3. Put a ball of newspaper in a square of brown paper. Tape it together. Tie it to the stick with string. Decorate your drum and play it!

INDEX

Entries in *italics* are activity pages.

© 1996 Watts Books, London, New York, Sydney
All rights reserved. Printed in Malaysia. .
Published simultaneously in Canada
1 2 3 4 5 R 99 98 97 96 95 94

Editor: Annabel Martin
Consultant: Keith Lye
Design: Ruth Levy
Artwork: Cilla Eurich and Ruth Levy
Photographs: Peter Millard

First American Edition © 1996 by Children's Press
A Division of Grolier Publishing
Sherman Turnpike
Danbury, CT 06816

Hewitt, Sally.
    The Plains people / Sally Hewitt
        p.   cm. - (Footsteps in time)
   Summary: Describes the traditional way of life of the Indians of the Great Plains. Includes activities in which common items represent what the Indians used, such as making a buffalo skin tipi out of brown paper.
    ISBN 0-516-08073-3
   1. Indians of North America--Great Plains--Social life and customs--Juvenile literture. 2. Indians of North America--Great Plains--Material culture--Juvenile literature. 3. Creative activities and seat work--Juvenile literature. [1. Indians of North America--Great Plains--Social life and customs. 2. Handicraft.] I. Title. II. Series.
E99.G73H48 1996   95-25251
978'.00497--dc20   CIP AC